... IF YOU LIVED AT THE TIME OF THE
Civil War

by Kay Moore
illustrated by Anni Matsick

SCHOLASTIC INC.
New York   Toronto   London   Auckland   Sydney

For George D. and Mattie A. Canoles, who lived history and shared the past with a thankful granddaughter

ISBN 0-590-45422-6

Copyright © 1994 by Kay Moore.
Illustrations copyright © 1994 by Scholastic Inc.
All rights reserved. Published by Scholastic Inc.

30 29 28 27 26 25 24 23 22   2 3 4 5 6/0

Printed in the U.S.A.   23

First Scholastic printing, April 1994

Book design by Laurie McBarnette

CONTENTS

Introduction

Each day, decisions are made that touch you. Some you make, such as what you wear to school and eat for lunch. Some are made by others, such as when your mother makes a dentist appointment for you. You and your mother may not agree that you need to visit the dentist. What *you* believe is called your "point of view."

Having two different points of view does not mean that one person is all right and the other person all wrong. But deciding what point of view will be used is sometimes hard. Most problems can be solved by talking and each person giving in on some things. This is called a "compromise."

However, there are times in history when a compromise cannot easily be reached. People look at the same questions about life and their answers are different. This book is about one of those times when different points of view led to war.

It was a war that divided the nation. People had to decide whether to support the North or the South.

The war has been called the brothers' war because families fought on both sides. It also has been called the children's crusade because children as young as nine years old were part of it. It touched the lives of all who lived through it no matter what their age or where they lived. It changed life in the United States forever. It is known as the Civil War.

When was the Civil War fought?

The American Civil War can be measured in five Aprils. It began in April 1861, and ended in April 1865 when General Robert E. Lee, who led the Southern troops, surrendered to General Ulysses S. Grant, the commander of the Northern Army.

How did the war start?

Between November 1860, and March 1861, some of the states in the South decided that they didn't want to be part of the United States anymore. They wanted to be free to govern themselves.

The newly elected President, Abraham Lincoln, did not believe the Southern states had the right to *secede from*—leave—the Union. But South Carolina withdrew and tried to take over Fort Sumter, a United States fort in the harbor of Charleston. Since the fort was in the

South, Southerners felt it belonged to them. But the Union soldiers would not leave, so Southern troops fired cannons at the fort. It was April 12, 1861.

After this attack, President Lincoln ordered Northern troops to prepare for war.

Many Southern men left the Union Army to join the Southern Army, and the Civil War began.

Why did the Southern states want to leave the Union?

Many families in the South lived on large farms called plantations, where they grew crops like cotton and rice. They needed a lot of people to work on the plantations. Ever since 1619, workers had been brought from Africa. Ships had gone across the ocean where black men, women, and children were taken against their will and sold as slaves when they arrived in America. Slaves had no rights, and they had to do what their owners told them to do.

The South depended on slaves to work on their huge farms. Crops were the main business. By the 1800s there were few slaves in the North. Many Northerners did not believe it was right to buy and sell human beings, and industry—not farming—was important. The Southern states were afraid that the government in Washington, D.C., would take away their right to own slaves and to set up their own rules.

The South did not like the name Civil War. To them this meant that they had done something wrong by leaving the Union. They felt they had the right to leave and set up their own governments.

Southerners used many names for the war instead of Civil War. The War Between the States was heard most often.

Which states left the Union?

Eleven states left the United States to form a confederacy—a group of states that works together but allows each state to keep its own laws. There are no laws that all the states must follow.

South Carolina was the first, followed by Alabama, Florida, Texas, Georgia, Louisiana, and Mississippi.

After the takeover of Fort Sumter, four more states—Arkansas, North Carolina, Virginia, and Tennessee—joined the new nation. All together they were called the Confederate States of America.

There were nine million people in these states, three million of them slaves.

Which states stayed in the Union?

If you lived in Maine, New Hampshire, Vermont, Massachusetts, Rhode Island, Connecticut, New York, New Jersey, Pennsylvania, Ohio, Delaware, Indiana, Illinois, Michigan, Wisconsin, Minnesota, Iowa, or Kansas, you lived in a state that stayed in the Union. The border states of Missouri, Maryland, and Kentucky also stayed in the Union, but many residents sided with the South. The western part of Virginia felt strong ties to the North, broke away, and became the state of West Virginia. California and Oregon remained loyal to the North.

There were twenty-two million people in these states, including a few slaves. There were many people who were new to America. They had left Europe to find a better life.

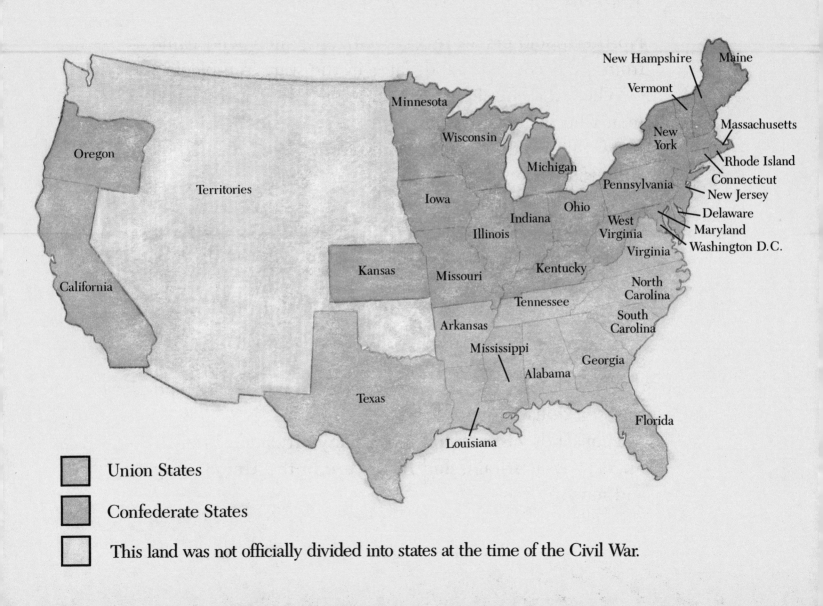

Minnesota

New Hampshire　　　Maine

Vermont

Wisconsin

New
York

Michigan

Massachusetts

Oregon

Rhode Island

Territories

Pennsylvania

Connecticut
New Jersey

Iowa

Ohio

Delaware

Indiana

West
Virginia

Maryland

Illinois

Washington D.C.

California

Kansas

Missouri

Kentucky

Virginia

North
Carolina

Tennessee

South
Carolina

Arkansas

Mississippi

Georgia

Alabama

Texas

Florida

Louisiana

Union States

Confederate States

This land was not officially divided into states at the time of the Civil War.

Who fought in the Northern Army?

Northern soldiers were U.S. citizens, men who came from other countries and, later in the war, free blacks.

When the war began, the regular army had 16,000 men who had enlisted for five years. President Lincoln knew this wouldn't be enough, so he asked for 75,000 volunteers for ninety days.

As the war continued, men stopped volunteering. The government started offering money to join the army. In 1863, the Union began drafting anyone between twenty and forty-five years old.

Most soldiers were between sixteen and thirty years old. Many were unmarried because married men were often able to buy a substitute or pay a three hundred dollar fee so they didn't have to fight. A private was paid thirteen dollars a month.

Thousands of men from Germany, Ireland, France, Spain, Great Britain, and Italy were in the Union army and navy.

Who fought in the Southern Army?

The South did not have an army or navy at the beginning of the war, only small state units. The President of the Confederate States, Jefferson Davis, called for 100,000 volunteers, and many men responded. Few had any military training. Most had been farmers before the war.

The South found it needed to draft men to fight in 1862. All men between eighteen and thirty-five were ordered into the army for the length of the war, but owners of twenty or more slaves didn't have to fight. Substitutes were allowed until 1863. A private earned eleven dollars a month, but men often went a year without getting paid.

There were not as many soldiers from other countries in the Confederacy. Many of these were French. Native Americans, including Creeks, Cherokees, and Seminoles, formed whole Southern regiments. In March, 1865, the Confederacy passed a law allowing slaves in the army. But the war ended in April, so this never happened.

What was the Union Army Like?

The troops of the North were called Union, Federal, or Yankee, and mostly wore blue uniforms. During the war, they usually named the battles they fought after streams (such as Antietam Creek and Stone's River). They used maps in planning their movements, and rivers were easy landmarks to find.

The Union Armies were also named for rivers. The most famous was the Army of the Potomac.

The Union flag was the Stars and Stripes. It had thirty-four stars that represented all of the states in the United States before the war began. When the Southern states decided to leave the Union, President Lincoln did not allow the stars for those states to be removed from the flag. A star for West Virginia was added when that state was admitted to the Union.

What was the Confederate Army like?

The troops of the South were called Confederate or Rebel, and mostly wore gray uniforms (although these were more butternut, a brown color due to the dyes used). They usually named their battles after cities (such as Sharpsburg and Murfreeboro) because most battles took place in the South and the soldiers knew the land where the fighting was happening.

Southern Armies were generally named for states, such as the Army of Northern Virginia and the Army of Tennessee.

The first Confederate flag was called the Stars and Bars, but later the Rebel Flag was adopted.

Would you have seen a battle in the North?

If you stayed at home in the North, you probably wouldn't have seen a battle. Except for a few raids and some fighting in the western border states, Southern troops fought little on Northern lands. They felt it was their duty to defend their own land rather than attack the North. Two major battles of the war were fought in the Northern states near Sharpsburg, Maryland, and Gettysburg, Pennsylvania.

You may have seen a battle if you were a bugler in the Army like nine-year-old Jimmy Dugan. His main job was to be the camp alarm clock, sounding calls for drills and meals. He also did other tasks like cutting hair and running errands. Johnny Clem was a ten-year-old drummer boy who became known as "Johnny Shiloh" during that battle. He was given the title of lance sergeant, and went on to become a soldier, being hurt twice. Other boys were powder monkeys in the Navy. They had to

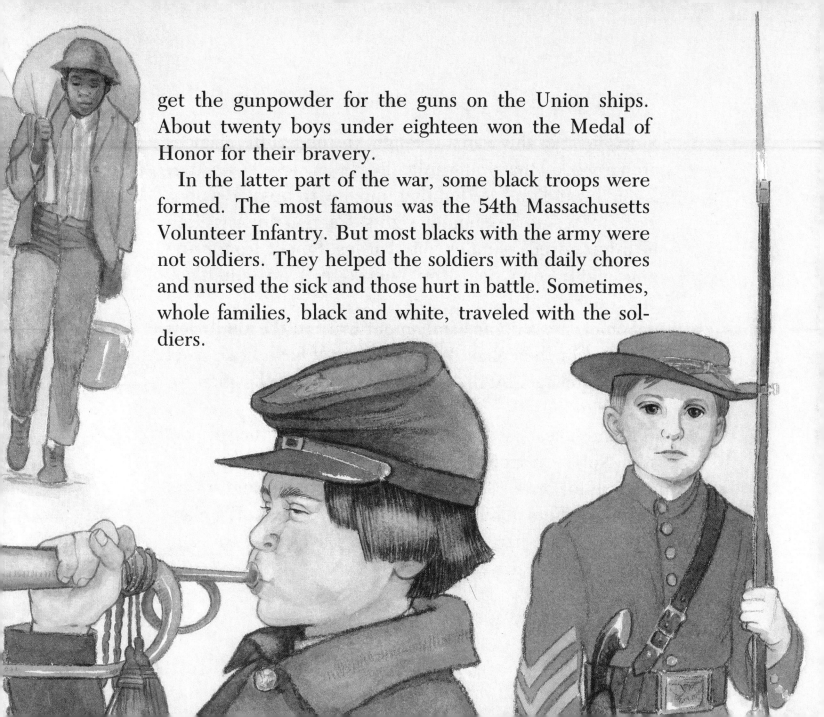

get the gunpowder for the guns on the Union ships. About twenty boys under eighteen won the Medal of Honor for their bravery.

In the latter part of the war, some black troops were formed. The most famous was the 54th Massachusetts Volunteer Infantry. But most blacks with the army were not soldiers. They helped the soldiers with daily chores and nursed the sick and those hurt in battle. Sometimes, whole families, black and white, traveled with the soldiers.

Would you have seen a battle in the South?

Since most of the war was fought in the South, chances are very good that you would have been close to a battle. Even if you didn't see fighting, moving troops and troops in camps would be common sights. Cannon fire was often heard hundreds of miles from battles. Smoke from firing guns and burning fields could get so thick it would block out the sun.

Sometimes a home came under fire and the family left it or hid in the cellar. Your home may have been used as headquarters by the army officers or as a hospital for the wounded.

Male slaves may have been forced to help the soldiers stop Northern troops by digging pits and building dirt mounds for protection. Women slaves cooked and sewed for the soldiers. Children helped their parents. If a plantation became part of a battlefield, slaves took cover in the forests or ran away.

While eighteen was the enlistment age at the start of the war, some Southern boys couldn't wait. One story tells of a boy who felt it was wrong to lie about his age. So he wrote the number *18* on a piece of paper and put the paper in the sole of his shoe. This let him truthfully answer that he was over *18*! Later, the Confederate government passed a law that let younger boys enlist. Boys as young as eleven joined.

The Cadets of the Virginia Military Institute, ages fourteen to eighteen, helped win the Battle of New Market, Virginia. Southern soldiers came from families who had lived in the South for many years.

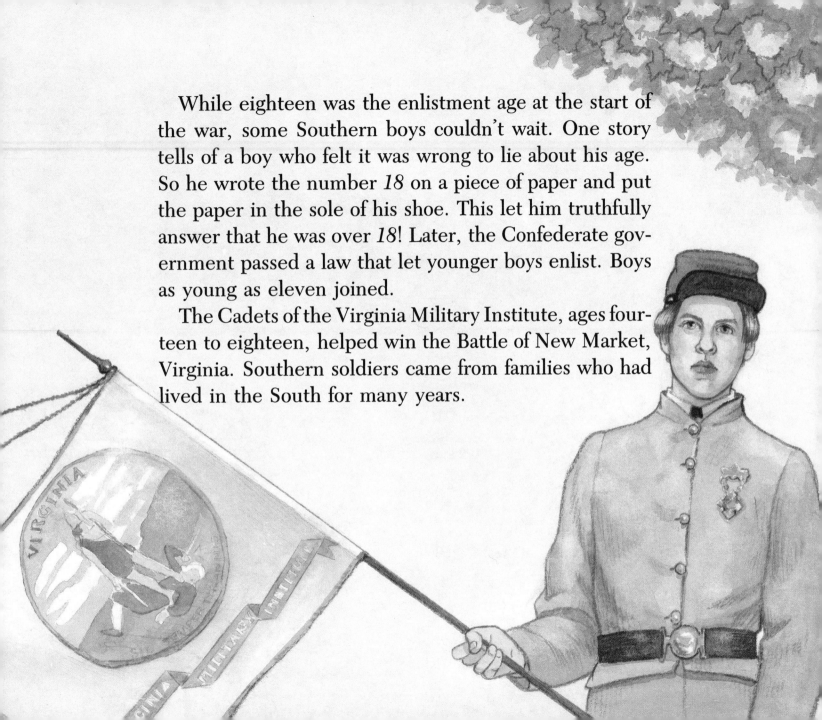

Did your home life in the North change because of the war?

The kind of life that you led before the war continued. People still farmed in the country. In the cities, there were a large number of factories and businesses. If your family owned a farm or business, it may have made more money by selling food, clothing, and weapons to the army. You would have lived in a big house and enjoyed parties and dances. You could buy fancy food and special clothes.

Favorite children's clothes looked like army uniforms. Eight-year-old Tad Lincoln had a small-size colonel's uniform and other children had Zouave jackets (a colorful soldier's uniform). For many in the North, the push to supply the soldiers during the war helped them get rich.

If your family didn't have much money or worked for someone else, the war did make your hard life worse. With higher prices for food and housing and often lower wages, everyone in a family had to work even harder to get money to live. Women took jobs when men left to fight.

You always thought and worried about your family, if they were in the army. But the fighting was going on far away. It did not make your life very different.

Did your home life in the South change because of the war?

Life was very different than before the war. Most of the battles were fought in the South. There were Union ships blockading the Southern coastal towns. Everyday items could not be gotten. You had to make do with things that you had and you used items in many different ways.

Cloth was made by spinning and knitting homespun wool. Neatly cut thorns became sewing pins. Dried persimmon seeds were made into buttons. Plants and vegetables were used for dyes. Onion skins make things a brownish-orange color, and carrot tops turn items greenish yellow. Patchwork clothes and quilts were used in all houses. When the feet wore out on a pair of socks, the tops were carefully unwoven, the thread twisted on a spinning wheel, and then knitted into new stockings or gloves. Hats were made by weaving corn husks, palmetto leaves, or other grasses.

With the men away at the war, life changed. If you

had chores before the war, you had more now. Even very young children had chores to do, from planting and weeding the garden to washing dishes.

If you lived in a large plantation home, your life stayed almost the same while the slaves stayed. House slaves helped with the cooking, cleaning, and washing. Field slaves planted a garden and tended the crops. But as the Union Army moved through the South, many slaves left with them or refused to work for the family anymore. For slaves the war was an opportunity to escape to the North.

Southern women and children had to provide for themselves, something they were not used to doing.

Did you continue to go to school in the North?

Most Northern children continued to go to public school during the war. You would be in school from 8 A.M. to 5 P.M. You'd spend your day reading from a McGuffey Reader, doing "sums" and writing on a slate, and memorizing "pieces" to say out loud.

The war did affect the schools when schoolmasters were drafted. Women took over as teachers or the school was closed. Illinois teachers had to take a loyalty oath before they could teach. This meant they had to swear that they believed in the Union. They would only teach things that supported the Union side of the war.

Some children, especially those who had come from Europe, worked in the factories with their parents. The work was hard and the pay poor. But the family needed the money so there was no choice, even if the child would have wanted to go to school.

Sometimes, boys took vacations from school to visit their fathers in the army. If you were twelve-year-old Fred Grant, you weren't in school in 1863 but with your father, General Ulysses S. Grant, as he worked to capture Vicksburg, Mississippi. Often, the boys stayed on by joining the army.

Did you continue to go to school in the South?

Before the war, there were not as many schools in the South as in the North and these were mostly private schools. If your parents had the money, you were educated at home with a tutor or a governess and then sent to a private high school. Some children were taught at home by family members.

Black children were seldom taught how to read or write. However, some children learned from watching their white playmates. Frederick Douglass, who became a well-known speaker against slavery as an adult, bought secret lessons with pieces of bread from poor neighborhood white boys when he was a house slave in Baltimore. He believed that learning to read was important in his desire to be free, but he was caught and punished many times while he was learning.

Slaves who knew how to read and write taught others in "pit schools"—holes in the ground hidden so they wouldn't be found.

When war began, most tutors became soldiers. Staying alive became more important than education to many families. You may have done farm work and chores around the house rather than study. Women kept a few schools open and newly printed textbooks soon showed Southern spirit. You could have practiced number problems in which Confederate soldiers whipped Yankees. But many schools closed until the end of the war. Some schools were used as hospitals for the wounded soldiers or prisons for captured soldiers.

Was it hard to get food in the North?

Food prices went higher and some families were not able to buy much. Wages for most workers were about $2.50 to $3.00 a day. A workday was ten to twelve hours.

During the war, eggs cost as much as six dollars a dozen and bacon cost fifteen cents a pound. Prices rose as much as 75%. Rice, sweet potatoes, citrus fruits, and pecans were hard to find since food from the South did not come North.

Most meals were meat and potatoes. Boiled chicken or beef was often eaten with Irish potatoes. A plate of beans, potatoes, ham or corned beef, bread, and coffee would cost fifteen cents.

Food was often fried in butter, lard, or bacon grease. Vegetables were well cooked, with corn being the most popular. Fruit was eaten at every meal. Desserts such as cake and pie were very well liked.

For most families, the main meal of the day was eaten at noon. Children came from school and the father came from work for dinner. Supper would be a lighter meal such as cold meat, potato salad, and fresh fruit, and would be eaten at six o'clock. If a family worked and could not get home at noon, supper became the main meal.

The business of canning food was started at this time. Soldiers were given canned food when on the march. Sometimes they brought a tin home for their families to try. Canned milk was a very new thing. Canned fruit like peaches or cherries was a treat in winter.

Sometimes, families or soldiers ran out of food, but neighbors and churches would help. The Sanitary Commission was a special group started by the government to help soldiers.

Was it hard to get food in the South?

Food was harder to get as the war went on and on. Union soldiers, called bummers, sometimes took food and livestock from Southern families or ruined their fields and gardens.

Meat was the hardest thing to get since much of it came from hunting. It was also hard to keep. Some meat was cut into strips and sun-dried. Meat was also salted and smoked. Salt was made by boiling salt water or digging up the dirt under smokehouses. The salt that had fallen off other smoked meat was taken from the dried soil.

Things that were grown or gathered were the main foods of most people. Tea was made from the dried leaves of berries. Coffee was made by boiling grain like wheat or corn. Baking soda, which was used to make bread, was made from the ashes of corncobs. Molasses or honey was used instead of sugar. The *Confederate Receipt Book* gave many hints for what to use for food.

Your family may have eaten only one to two small meals per day so that the food would last as long as possible. Slaves that worked in the house could get leftovers. Field workers were given very small portions of meat and cornmeal. But this wasn't much food after working hard from sunrise to sunset.

How did you entertain yourself in the North?

There was always a lot to do if you lived in a city like New York. The circus was often in town. There were special musical shows called minstrel shows. P.T. Barnum's American Museum of Unusual Sights was well liked. Everyone liked vaudeville shows where dancing, comedy, and singing were done along with a play. Tickets were bought for fifteen cents.

The war also inspired new kinds of events. The Sanitary Commission had fairs to raise money to help the soldiers. Exhibits of captured battle flags and other military items brought huge crowds. Parades were often seen as men marched off to battle.

Baseball became popular. Soldiers learned and played the game to pass the time between battles. They taught the game to their children when they came home to visit.

Farm fairs were held in the country. But they showed guns and war materials as well as fruits and vegetables. Swimming, fishing, footraces, horse racing, wrestling, and shooting matches were favorite things to do.

Songs like the "Battle Hymn of the Republic" and "Battle Cry of Freedom" were sung all over the North where people got together, especially at the Fourth of July parade and celebration. Toys like guns and drums were very popular.

How did you entertain yourself in the South?

There was very little time to play due to chores. You liked games such as "Hi, Spy," "Blind Man's Buff," and "Fox and Geese." Of course, playing war was a favorite.

When others couldn't join the fun, boys passed the time by swinging on a grapevine or tooting on a whittled flute. Girls had tea with rag doll or corn shuck friends. Store-bought dolls were almost never seen. Playing checkers by firelight ended many long, tiring days. Singing or whistling tunes, such as "When Johnny Comes Marching Home" or "Bonnie Blue Flag" made children feel close to their fathers and brothers.

From around six years old, black children were expected to work. You could put the animals in the barn, clean the yard around the house, or run errands, until you were old enough to work in the fields. Unless you were told to play with the children of the family, you were punished if you were found playing during the day. At night, you were usually too tired to play.

Black children sang the songs they heard their parents sing while they worked. "Swing Low, Sweet Chariot" and "Follow the Drinking Gourd" helped them pass the long days.

How did you support the war in the North?

While money was given when possible, you probably helped in other ways.

Girls helped sew hundreds of towels and knit socks. They scraped lint from cloth that was used to make bandages. Boys used wheelbarrows and wagons to haul things to the packinghouse. Potatoes and onions were taken from gardens and sent to the soldiers to help prevent a disease called scurvy. (This happens when not enough Vitamin C is eaten.) Boys also helped wives of men who had enlisted by sawing firewood. On farms, boys helped with animals and crop harvest.

Some older children may have helped their parents run a station on the Underground Railroad. This wasn't a real railroad. It was the secret way to get from the South and slavery to the North and freedom. People who helped the slaves escape were called railroad workers.

How did you support the war in the South?

When Southern soldiers passed by, your family shared food and gave whatever clothing you could spare. Officers may have stayed in your home or come to dinner. Southern women made uniforms for the soldiers and knit clothes. Families close to hospitals helped the wounded.

You helped by not wasting anything. If the weather was warm, you didn't wear shoes—that saved leather. Endpapers were cut from books and used as writing paper. Envelopes were turned inside out and used again. You wore clothes that were too small or too large and always patched. You searched your neighborhood for berries, nuts, and other food that could stretch your family's diet. You ate less and didn't complain because you knew food was getting harder to find.

Male slaves were often taken from the plantations by the army to help build war defenses. This meant that the slaves left had to work extra hard to get all the work done, or it was left undone. Family members also had to start doing daily chores.

How did you get news from the front lines in the North?

Before the war, letters would come to the post office or general store and you would have to pick up your mail. With so many families writing to soldiers, two big changes happened in the Union's mail. First, mail was divided into classes. First class was for letters, second class was for newspapers, and third class was for magazines. The price of postage was by class. Before the war the price was for how far the item had to travel. Second, mail delivery to the home began in large cities. Letter carriers or "postmen" took letters right to your door.

Late in the war, Union soldiers who wanted to send money home safely could use a postal money order, like a bank check. The receiver could take the money order to the local post office and get money in return.

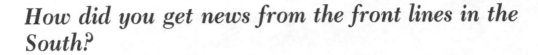

How did you get news from the front lines in the South?

Getting news about the war or your family in the South was very hard. Often you waited months, sometimes years, to hear news of your family members. Telegraph lines were often cut. Mail that did make it through the lines had to be picked up at the post office or general store, which was often a long walk or ride. Soldiers carrying letters for friends may not have arrived.

As long as there was still a supply of newsprint, newspapers like the Vicksburg *Citizen* and the Richmond *Enquirer* followed the battles and printed the names of soldiers who were killed, wounded, or captured. Since many people couldn't read, often someone read the news aloud in a public place. Later, newspapers were printed on wallpaper or wrapping paper.

Abraham Lincoln

William T. Sherman

Who were the famous people you would hear about in the North?

Everyone talked about President Abraham Lincoln and the way he was running the war. Lincoln had grown a beard because eleven-year-old Grace Bedell told him he would look better with one. He worked closely with many army generals including George B. McClellan, Ambrose Burnside, George Meade, Ulysses S. Grant, and William T. Sherman.

George B. McClellan

Ulysses S. Grant

Sojourner Truth

Frederick Douglass

When Lincoln met Harriet Beecher Stowe, who wrote *Uncle Tom's Cabin*, a book that showed the evils of slavery, he is said to have called her "the little woman who made this big war."

Escaped slaves like Sojourner Truth and Frederick Douglass gave talks to tell people to fight for the freedom of the slaves. Colonel Robert Gould Shaw led the most well-known black army unit, the 54th Massachusetts Volunteer Infantry.

Robert Gould Shaw

Harriet Beecher Stowe

Mathew Brady's photographs let those at home see these people. Photography was new so people wanted to see the real battlefield pictures. Photographers followed the army in wagons that became traveling darkrooms.

Another kind of art was made by Thomas Nast. He made drawings of a fat, jolly Santa Claus in a sleigh filled with toys. They took people's thoughts away from the war and began a holiday tradition.

Women were very busy helping the sick and wounded at the battlefields and in government hospitals. Dorothea Dix set up a group of nurses. They were paid forty cents per day by the government. Clara Barton took food and medicine right to the battle lines. Dr. Mary Walker became the first woman officer in the U.S. Army. She was awarded the Congressional Medal of Honor for her bravery.

Who were the famous people you would hear about in the South?

Every child in the South knew of Jefferson Davis and General Robert E. Lee. You knew Davis had been elected the President of the Confederacy and that he chose Lee to lead the Southern troops.

Lee had resigned from the Northern Army when Virginia left the Union. He made the battle plans and led his troops on his horse, Traveler. While he was a great soldier, he really didn't like fighting. He loved his family and enjoyed having his feet tickled by his children when he read them stories. Lee was greatly admired by all Southerners.

"Stonewall" Jackson, "Jeb" Stuart, James Longstreet, A. P. Hill, John Mosby, and Nathan Bedford Forrest were other well-known soldiers.

White and black people had heard of the person called Moses who worked on the Underground Railroad. This wasn't a real railroad. It was the secret code name for any route from the South to freedom in the North.

Many people helped slaves leave the South for the Northern states or Canada. Slave catchers, men who caught runaway slaves, tried to locate Moses and stop this from happening. Slaves waited for the call that it was time to go. Few knew that Moses was really Harriet Tubman, herself an escaped slave from Maryland. She led thousands of people out of the South to the North. She also went into the South toward the end of the war to let slaves know that they had been freed by the Emancipation Proclamation, which President Lincoln had signed in January, 1863.

What words and expressions came from life in the North?

General Ambrose Burnside, who wore bushy side whiskers, was the model for the style known as *sideburns*. In 1861, the government printed money called *greenbacks* because of the ink color. Bummers, who were soldiers who roamed the countryside looking for food and valuables, has been shortened to our present *bums*.

The word *mailman* became common when free home delivery of the mail in the cities was started. Women started to use the word *shampoo* when they washed their hair. The *chignon* became a popular way for women to wear their hair. The hair is wrapped into a knot at the back of the head. This is a plain style and women thought it would show their dedication to the war effort.

What words and expressions came from life in the South?

The term *Dixie* was a nickname for the South before the war. It may have started because of the Mason-Dixon line that divides Pennsylvania and Maryland. Another story is that it came from the ten-dollar bill, which was marked *Dix*, French for ten. Those in the Mississippi riverboat business called the bills Dixies, and the place where they came from Dixieland. The song "I Wish I Was in Dixie's Land" ("Dixie," for short) was played as Jefferson Davis became President of the Confederacy, and it became a symbol for the South.

At the end of the war, the North set up the governments in the defeated Southern states. Southerners who worked with these new governments were called *scalawags*. Northerners who came South to sell needed items at high prices or control the votes of the former slaves were called *carpetbaggers* due to their traveling bags made of carpetlike material.

How did life in the North change after the War?

There were about 360,000 casualties on the Union side of the war. If your family had lost a loved one, you still felt the pain. The end of the war brought good things for some people and more loss for others. There were more factories than before the war so there were more jobs. These were often given to returning soldiers, so many women left the work force. Women who still held jobs were paid less than the men workers.

Newly invented machines, such as grain mowers and reapers, made farming easier and clothing could be produced faster with sewing machines.

Companies grew larger. Their low-pay workers felt they could strike for more money and end the fourteen-hour workday. Going on strike was unpatriotic during the war.

Many freed slaves moved into the North and only found low-paying jobs.

President Lincoln hoped for a quick and peaceful re-union of the Southern states to the Union. He wanted to make the "divided house" whole. Others in government felt the South needed to be punished. Lincoln was assassinated before his wishes for pardoning the Southern states could come true. Andrew Johnson then became president. He was not able to do what Lincoln had planned. The Northern states gained a lot of power in the government. But it was at the cost of many lives.

How did life in the South change after the War?

There were about 260,000 casualties on the side of the South. It took a long time for the South to recover from the ruin of the war. Cities and towns had to be rebuilt. Farmland had to be reworked and planted without the use of slaves. Railroad and telegraph lines needed to be reset. People had to live with little or no money and few belongings. The war had touched your life every day for four years. It was hard to believe it was really over.

The people who had been slaves also had to make big adjustments. The Emancipation Proclamation had given them freedom, but life was hard. Most ex-slaves had no education and had little or no money. Schools and other public places were still divided by color. Some freed blacks worked for their former owners for money. But others left for the North where they hoped to get their own land.

Many people from the North came South at the end of the war. Some came to teach the freed slaves. But others came to control and punish according to the Reconstruction Act passed by the North. The Union Army took over the government. The South was treated like a hated enemy. This was what Lincoln had not wanted to happen.

The hardest and slowest thing to change were people's feelings. Losing made Southerners accept the power of the national government. You were part of the whole. You also had to recognize that the slaves were free and had the same rights of citizenship. Your world changed a lot during the war and life was never the same again.